Macmillan/M[...]
Matter[...]

Molly's Magnet

AUTHORS

Mary Atwater
The University of Georgia
Prentice Baptiste
University of Houston
Lucy Daniel
Rutherford County Schools
Jay Hackett
University of Northern Colorado

Richard Moyer
University of Michigan, Dearborn
Carol Takemoto
Los Angeles Unified School District
Nancy Wilson
Sacramento Unified School District

Macmillan/McGraw-Hill School Publishing Company
New York   Columbus

Molly's Magnet

Themes:
Systems and Interactions / Energy

Lessons

Activities!

EXPLORE

TRY THIS

Getting Stuck

Molly was too young to play with the older children. She was too old to play with the younger children.

Theme **T** SYSTEMS and INTERACTIONS

Most of the time, Molly played by herself. Then she found a treasure and she was never alone again.

Molly found a big magnet and put it in her pocket. What do you think Molly can do with her magnet? Help her do the activity on the next page.

Activity!

What Will Stick to a Magnet?

You can find out some things Molly's magnet will do.

What You Need

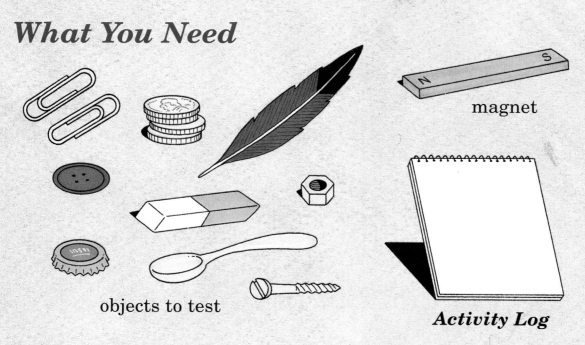

magnet

objects to test

Activity Log

What To Do

1. Make one group of objects you think will stick to a magnet.

2. Make another group of objects you think won't stick to a magnet.

3. Test the objects with the magnet.

4. Make new groups after you have tested all the objects.

What Happened?

1. Tell why you think some objects stuck to the magnet and other objects didn't.

2. Draw a picture of both groups of objects in your *Activity Log*.

What Sticks to a Magnet?

Molly noticed that all kinds of things stuck to her **magnet.** "This is great!" thought Molly. "Maybe a pizza will stick to my magnet, too."

Minds On! What kinds of things stuck to Molly's magnet? Do you think a pizza will stick to it? Why or why not? ●

No matter how close Molly stood to the pizza store, nothing happened. She even tried holding her magnet up to the store window.

Activity!

Will a Magnet Stick Through Some Things?

What You Need

magnet

paper clip

paper

cloth

waxed paper

foil

Activity Log

Wrap the magnet in the paper. Put the paper clip on your desk. Touch the paper-wrapped magnet to the paper clip. Does the paper clip stick to the magnet through the paper? Remove the paper and try the cloth. Then try the foil and the waxed paper. Write which things the magnet will stick through in your *Activity Log.*

Molly went home. She was hungry and went to the refrigerator to get an apple. That's when it happened. WHUMP! Molly was stuck to the refrigerator.

She had to give a good strong tug on the magnet to pull it loose. Molly's mother smiled at her. "I guess the steel in the refrigerator was **attracted** by your magnet, Molly. That's why you stuck so hard."

Molly looked all around. There were other magnets on the refrigerator. She had never had trouble pulling any of these magnets away from the refrigerator. Why was her new magnet so hard to pull away? Do the next activity to help Molly find out.

Activity!

Are Some Magnets Stronger Than Others?

What You Need

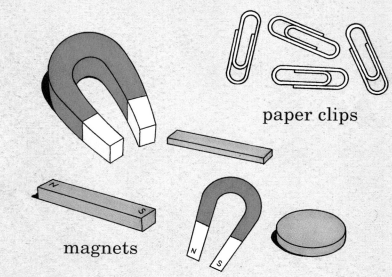

paper clips

magnets

Activity Log

What To Do

1. Use one magnet at a time.
2. Put the magnet into a pile of paper clips.
3. Carefully pick up the magnet. Pull off each paper clip. Count the paper clips.
4. Try each magnet. Record the number of paper clips each magnet holds in your ***Activity Log.***

Which magnet was strongest?

How do you know?

Molly's mother began to make lunch. She showed Molly that the can opener uses a magnet to attract the lid from a can that is being opened. "Stay away from cans," laughed her mother.

Molly walked around her house looking for other things that use magnets. She found a few things in the kitchen. She found some things in her toy box. She even found some things in a tool box.

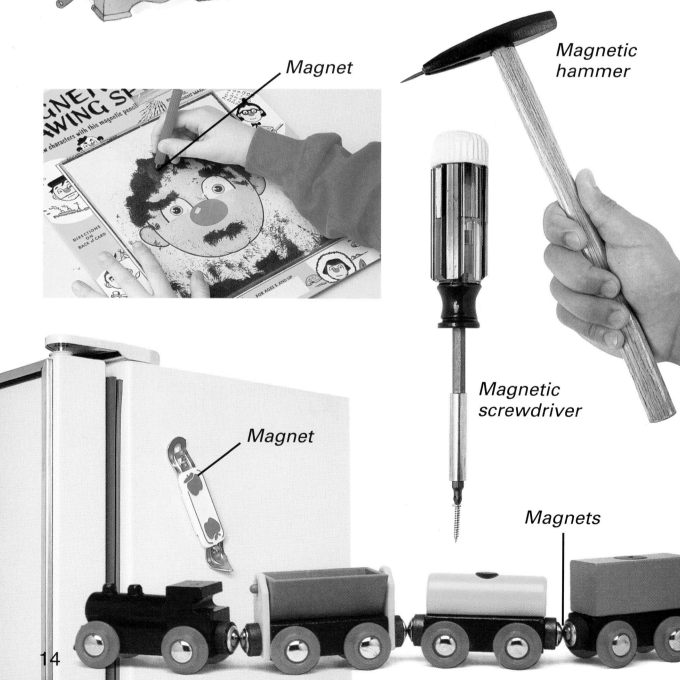

Magnet

Magnetic hammer

Magnetic screwdriver

Magnet

Magnets

Molly's mother told her about some magnets that are very strong. "Do you think your magnet is strong enough to pick up a car?" laughed her mother.

SCIENCE TECHNOLOGY AND Society

Focus on Technology

Magnets at Work

This machine uses electricity to make a very strong magnet. When the electricity is on, the magnet will attract the metal. To drop the metal, the operator will turn off the electricity.

Opposites Attract

Molly went out to play. There she saw a magnet that looked like hers. Molly took her magnet out of her pocket. She reached for the other magnet. When she got close, the other magnet moved away from hers.

Theme **T** ENERGY

Molly chased the magnet. "I'll sneak around and get it from the other side," she said. Suddenly the two magnets clanked together. "Why did that happen?" she thought. Do the next activity to help her find out.

Activity!

When Do Magnets Attract Each Other?

Do magnets attract everything? Do they attract each other? Find out in this activity.

What You Need

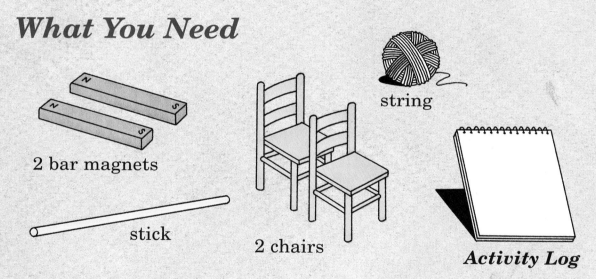

2 bar magnets

stick

2 chairs

string

Activity Log

What To Do

1. Tie the string to one magnet. Hang the magnet from the stick.

2. Hold the other magnet in your hand. Hold one end of your magnet up to each end of the hanging magnet. Record what happens in your *Activity Log.*

3. Hold the other end of your magnet up to each end of the hanging magnet. Record what happens.

What Happened?

1. Which ends of the magnets were attracted?

2. Which ends weren't attracted?

3. What happened when the ends weren't attracted?

Which Ends Attract?

Molly wanted to keep the new magnet, too. She tried to put both magnets in her pocket, but they wouldn't behave. Molly put both magnets on the ground. The magnets looked almost alike.

Both had an **N** on one end and an **S** on the other. When Molly put the **N** of one magnet near the **S** of the other, the magnets would attract each other and stick together.

But when she tried to put both ends marked **N** or both ends marked **S** together, the magnets would **repel** each other and scoot apart.

"If I put these magnets in my pocket in just the right way, I can keep them both," thought Molly. So she took them both and began to walk toward the park.

Minds On! How do you think she put them in her pocket? •

Molly thought about the magnets in her pocket. She wondered what magnets are used for besides attracting objects. Do the activity to see.

Activity!

The Main Attraction

What You Need

bar magnet   string   stick   books   *Activity Log*

What To Do

1. Put the books on a desk. Place the stick under them so that it is over the floor.

2. Tie the string to the magnet. Hang the magnet from the stick.

3. Let the magnet swing freely. Watch what happens. Write about it in your *Activity Log.*

Which way did the magnet point when it stopped turning?

A magnet is used in a **compass**. This tool helps people find their way. Molly had seen a compass in a car.

23

Magnet Power

Next, Molly saw David and Kim playing in the sand. Molly showed them her magnets.

"May I use one of your magnets, Molly?" asked Kim. Molly handed her a magnet. Then David wanted one, too. Molly did not want to give away both of her magnets. Could she find a way to give a magnet to David, too? Do the next activity to find out.

Activity!

Can You Make a Magnet?

You will try to make some objects into magnets.

What You Need

bar magnet

small paper clips

steel nail

pencil

large paper clip

Activity Log

What To Do

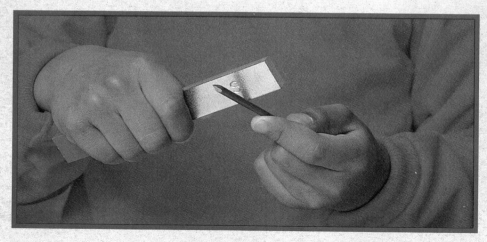

1. Rub one end of the magnet along the nail. Rub 50 times in the same direction.

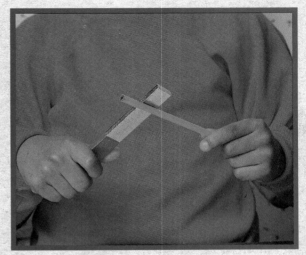

2. Use the end of the nail to see if it will pick up one small paper clip. Two small paper clips? Three small paper clips? Record what happened in your **Activity Log.**

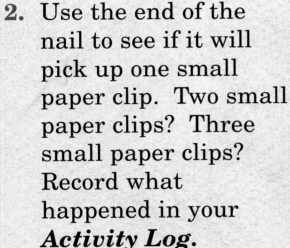

3. Can you make a pencil into a magnet? Now do steps 1 and 2 again with the pencil.

4. Can you make a paper clip into a magnet? Do steps 1 and 2 again with the large paper clip.

What Happened?

1. Which objects picked up paper clips?
2. How many did each object pick up?
3. Make a graph in your **Activity Log** to show how many objects were picked up.

Molly gave David a large paper clip. "Here," said Molly. "Rub this paper clip on my magnet and then you'll have a magnet, too."

"Thank you, Molly," David replied.

At the corner of the park, Molly saw some people. "What happened?" she asked Diego.

"Dr. Alvarez dropped her car keys down the drain and can't reach them," said Diego. Molly thought for a minute and smiled. The next activity will help you see what she thought.

Activity!

How Far Do Magnets Attract?

What You Need

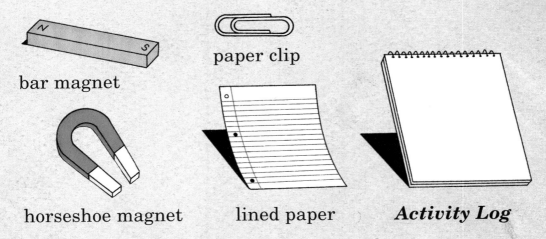

bar magnet

paper clip

horseshoe magnet

lined paper

Activity Log

What To Do

1. Put the paper clip on one line of the paper.

2. Start one of the magnets at the other end of the paper. Push it slowly toward the paper clip. Stop when the paper clip moves.

3. Count the number of lines between the magnet and the paper clip. Record this in your *Activity Log.*

4. Repeat steps 1 through 3 with the other magnet.

How many lines did you count each time?

Which magnet do you think is stronger? Why?

Molly went closer to the drain. She got a piece of string from David and Kim. She tied it around her magnet. Then she carefully lowered her magnet into the drain. **CLANK!** Molly slowly pulled the string up and there on the end of the magnet were the keys, two pieces of wire, and a bottle cap. "Thank you, Molly," said Dr. Alvarez. "I am so glad to have my keys back."

Molly went home with her magnet in her pocket. She thought about all she had done. She now knew that magnets were more than just toys. Dr. Alvarez had told her about magnets used in the hospital.

  ## Magnets in Medicine

Dr. Alvarez uses a machine to take pictures of the inside of a person's body. It uses a large magnet to take the pictures. Then Dr. Alvarez uses the pictures to help the person get well.

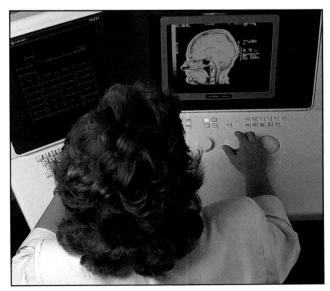

Vocabulary/Index